Unusual Birds

Jacqueline Dineen

OXFORD
UNIVERSITY PRESS

Contents

Introduction	3
How birds fly	4
Do all birds fly?	6
Do all birds make nests?	8
Where do cuckoos nest?	10
How do birds eat?	12
What a big beak!	14
Sleeping birds	16
Night hunters	18
The smallest bird	20
Pink flamingoes	22
Index	24

Introduction

There are many kinds of birds in the world.

What is the same about these birds?
What is different?

How birds fly

Birds have wings.
They flap their wings to take off and move forward.
They spread their wings out to glide through the air.

Most birds are light. They don't weigh very much. So when they flap their wings they can take off and fly.

wing

feathers

A bird's wing is made of thin bones and feathers.

Do all birds fly?

The ostrich is the biggest bird in the world. It is very heavy. It cannot fly but it can run very fast.

Ostriches have long, strong legs and very long necks.

Ostriches fight by kicking out with both feet.

Penguins cannot fly. They use their wings like flippers when they are swimming.

Do all birds make nests?

Many birds make nests. They lay their eggs in the nest.

Most birds keep their eggs warm in a nest until the chicks hatch out. Penguins do not make nests. The female lays one egg and the male penguin keeps it warm on its feet.

The eggs are kept warm under a fold of skin.

Where do cuckoos nest?

Cuckoos never make their own nests. They lay their eggs in the nests of other birds.

cuckoo egg

When the cuckoo chick hatches out, the other bird feeds it.

foster parent

cuckoo chick

This small bird is feeding a big cuckoo chick.

How do birds eat?

Birds eat food with their beaks. The shape of a bird's beak helps it to eat the food it likes.

crossbill

twisted beak

pine cone

The crossbill has a twisted beak so it can pick the seeds out of pine cones.

A nuthatch has a long beak. It can pick insects out of holes and cracks.

What a big beak!

This bird is a pelican. It has a beak shaped like a big spoon.

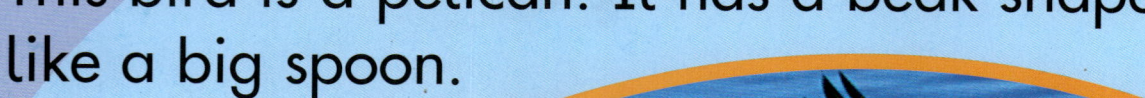

14

Pelicans eat lots of fish. They use their beaks like fishing nets.

A pelican can scoop up the fish with its big beak.

Sleeping birds

Many birds sleep in trees. They perch on the branches. They curl their feet round the branch and dig their claws in. This stops them falling off the branch when they are asleep.

A bird curls its foot round the branch and digs in its claws.

Birds hide among the leaves in trees. This helps to keep them safe when they are asleep.
Cats cannot find them easily.

Night hunters

Some birds sleep in the daytime. They fly at night. They go hunting for food.

Owls have big eyes so they can see in the dark. They hunt for food at night.

An owl can turn its head round to look backwards. It can turn its head upside down too.

The smallest bird

The hummingbird is the smallest bird in the world. It flaps its wings very fast so it can keep flying on one spot. It stays in the air like this while it feeds from flowers.

A hummingbird sips nectar from flowers with its long beak.

Nectar is sweet juice.

beak

flower head

21

Pink flamingoes

Flamingoes are pink because of the food they eat. They eat small water plants, shrimps and snails. This food has colouring in it.

Flamingoes stand in the water on their long legs. They scoop up food and water in their curved beaks.

Flamingoes have long necks and long legs.

Index

beak 12, 13, 14, 15, 20, 21, 23
chick 9, 11
crossbill 12
cuckoo 10, 11
eat 12, 15, 22
eggs 8, 9, 10
flamingoes 22, 23
fly 4, 5, 6, 7
hummingbird 20

nests 8, 9, 10
nuthatch 13
ostrich 6
owl 18, 19
pelican 14, 15
penguin 7, 9
sleep 16, 17
wings 4, 5, 7, 20